What Does the Bible Say About Sex?

Kay Arthur, David & BJ Lawson

PRECEPT MINISTRIES INTERNATIONAL

WATERBROOK
PRESS

WHAT DOES THE BIBLE SAY ABOUT SEX?
PUBLISHED BY WATERBROOK PRESS
12265 Oracle Boulevard, Suite 200
Colorado Springs, Colorado 80921

All Scripture quotations, unless otherwise indicated, are taken from the New American Standard Bible® (NASB), © Copyright The Lockman Foundation 1960, 1962, 1963, 1968, 1971, 1972, 1973, 1975, 1977, 1995. Used by permission. (www.Lockman.org). Scripture quotations marked (KJV) are taken from the King James Version.

Italics in Scripture quotations reflect the author's added emphasis.

ISBN 978-0-307-45771-4

Published in the United States by WaterBrook Multnomah, an imprint of the Crown Publishing Group, a division of Random House Inc., New York.

WATERBROOK and its deer colophon are registered trademarks of Random House Inc.

Printed in the United States of America
2009

10 9 8 7 6 5 4 3 2 1

SPECIAL SALES
Most WaterBrook Multnomah books are available at special quantity discounts when purchased in bulk by corporations, organizations, and special-interest groups. Custom imprinting or excerpting can also be done to fit special needs. For information, please e-mail SpecialMarkets@WaterBrookMultnomah.com or call 1-800-603-7051.

CONTENTS

This small-group study is for people who are interested in learning for themselves more about what the Bible says on various subjects, but who have only limited time to meet together. It's ideal, for example, for a lunch group at work, an early morning men's group, a young mothers' group meeting in a home, a Sunday-school class, or even family devotions. (It's also ideal for small groups that typically have longer meeting times—such as evening groups or Saturday morning groups—but want to devote only a portion of their time together to actual study, while reserving the rest for prayer, fellowship, or other activities.)

This book is designed so that all the group's participants will complete each lesson's study activities *at the same time.* Discussing your insights drawn from what God says about the subject reveals exciting, life-impacting truths.

Although it's a group study, you'll need a facilitator to lead the study and keep the discussion moving. (This person's function is *not* that of a lecturer or teacher. However, when this book is used in a Sunday-school class or similar setting, the teacher should feel free to lead more directly and to bring in other insights in addition to those provided in each week's lesson.)

If *you* are your group's facilitator, the leader, here are some helpful points for making your job easier:

- Go through the lesson and mark the text before you lead the group. This will give you increased familiarity with the material and will enable you to facilitate the group with greater ease. It may be easier for you to lead the group through the instructions for marking if you, as a leader, choose a specific color for each symbol you mark.

- As you lead the group, start at the beginning of the text and simply read it aloud in the order it appears in the lesson, including the "insight boxes," which appear throughout. Work through the lesson together, observing and discussing what you learn. As you read the Scripture verses, have the group say aloud the word they are marking in the text.

- The discussion questions are there simply to help you cover the material. As the class moves into the discussion, many times you will find that they will cover the questions on their own. Remember, the discussion questions are there to guide the group through the topic, not to squelch discussion.

- Remember how important it is for people to verbalize their answers and discoveries. This greatly strengthens their personal understanding of each week's lesson. Try to ensure that everyone has plenty of opportunity to contribute to each week's discussions.

- Keep the discussion moving. This may mean spending more time on some parts of the study than on others. If necessary, you should feel free to spread out a lesson over more than one session. However, remember that you don't want to slow the pace too much. It's much better to leave everyone "wanting more" than to have people dropping out because of declining interest.

- If the validity or accuracy of some of the answers seems questionable, you can gently and cheerfully remind the group to stay focused on the truth of the Scriptures. Your object is to learn what the Bible says, not to engage in human philosophy. Simply stick with the Scriptures and give God the opportunity to speak. His Word *is* truth (John 17:17)!

WHAT DOES THE BIBLE SAY ABOUT SEX?

Sex! Everyone is talking about it, yet many people are uncomfortable having honest conversations on this topic. If you bring God into the discussion, people often grow even more uncomfortable. Many find it hard to believe that God would care about this facet of their lives, while others resent what they see as interference with a private matter. Perhaps you are among those who consider their sexual behavior to be completely separate from their faith.

As our culture has grown more obsessed with sex, various misconceptions have cropped up, leaving people both inside and outside of the church confused and asking questions such as...

Why does God hate sex?

Does my choice of sexual expression really matter?

Whatever we do is okay as long as we love each other, right?

If love makes it okay, why do I sometimes feel guilty?

How far is too far if we're not married?

God has a lot to say in His Word about sex, both inside and outside of marriage. You may be surprised to learn that He is not antisex. On the contrary, He invented sex and values it so much that He wants to help us deal with it properly.

We will spend the next six weeks looking at what the Designer of sex says about His intention for this priceless gift.

Many people believe that sex is a physical need that must be fulfilled just as our need for food and water must be met. They consider it just another "animal appetite" to be satisfied, without any deeper spiritual meaning. In this lesson we'll look at the true origins of sex—who invented it, why it was created, and what boundaries, if any, were designed to protect it.

OBSERVE

Let's go back to the very beginning, to Genesis, the first book of the Bible, and see what God says about the first union between a man and a woman.

Leader: Read Genesis 1:25–28 aloud. Have the group say aloud and…

- *mark every reference to **God,** including pronouns such as **Our, Us,** and **His,** with a triangle, like this:* △
- *draw a box around every reference to **man,** including the pronouns **him** and **them:*** ☐

As you read the text, it's helpful to have the group say the key words aloud as they mark them. This way everyone will be sure they are marking every occurrence of the word,

GENESIS 1:25–28

25 God made the beasts of the earth after their kind, and the cattle after their kind, and everything that creeps on the ground after its kind; and God saw that it was good.

26 Then God said, "Let Us make man in Our image, according to Our likeness; and let them rule over the fish of the sea and over the birds of the sky and over the cattle and

over all the earth, and over every creeping thing that creeps on the earth."

27 God created man in His own image, in the image of God He created him; male and female He created them.

28 God blessed them; and God said to them, "Be fruitful and multiply, and fill the earth, and subdue it; and rule over the fish of the sea and over the birds of the sky and over every living thing that moves on the earth."

including any synonymous words or phrases. Do this throughout the study.

DISCUSS

• What did you learn from marking the references to man?

• Who created man?

• What specifically did you learn about the creation of man in verse 27?

• What is the first thing mankind was commanded to do in these verses?

• Is it possible to fulfill this command without sex?

• Is it possible in a same-sex union?

• Since God created mankind, who created sex?

• Logically then, who would determine the specifications and limitations of sex?

OBSERVE

Now let's look at Genesis 2, which offers a more detailed look at how man and woman were created.

Leader: Read aloud Genesis 2:7–8, 15–25. Have the group say aloud and...
- *draw a box around every reference to* **man,** *including pronouns.*
- *circle every reference to* (woman,) *including pronouns and synonyms such as* **wife.**

DISCUSS

- Discuss what you learned about the creation of man and woman in this passage.

- Who was created first?

GENESIS 2:7–8, 15–25

7 Then the LORD God formed man of dust from the ground, and breathed into his nostrils the breath of life; and man became a living being.

8 The LORD God planted a garden toward the east, in Eden; and there He placed the man whom He had formed....

15 Then the LORD God took the man and put him into the garden of Eden to cultivate it and keep it.

16 The LORD God commanded the man, saying, "From any tree of the garden you may eat freely;

17 but from the tree of the knowledge of good and evil you shall not eat, for in the day that you eat from it you will surely die."

18 Then the LORD God said, "It is not good for the man to be alone; I will make him a helper suitable for him."

19 Out of the ground the LORD God formed every beast of the field and every bird of the sky, and brought them to the man to see what he would call them; and whatever the man called a living creature, that was its name.

20 The man gave names to all the cattle, and to the birds of the

• Within a garden filled with so many good things, one thing was not good, according to verse 18. What was it?

• What was God's purpose for creating woman?

INSIGHT

The word translated as *helper* in this passage means "someone who comes alongside to help accomplish a task." It does not indicate someone of lesser value or position. As a matter of fact, the same Hebrew word used here often is used to describe God coming alongside us to deliver us from trouble. According to this passage, man needed a helper, a partner every bit his equal whose strengths would compensate for his weaknesses. She would be suitable for him, spiritually, emotionally, and physically.

• What was man's response to God's creation of woman?

• What did you learn from Genesis 2:24 about God's design for man and woman?

• Who is involved in becoming "one flesh"?

sky, and to every beast of the field, but for Adam there was not found a helper suitable for him.

21 So the LORD God caused a deep sleep to fall upon the man, and he slept; then He took one of his ribs and closed up the flesh at that place.

22 The LORD God fashioned into a woman the rib which He had taken from the man, and brought her to the man.

23 The man said, "This is now bone of my bones, and flesh of my flesh; she shall be called Woman, because she was taken out of Man."

24 For this reason a man shall leave his father and his mother, and be joined to his wife; and they shall become one flesh.

25 And the man and his wife were both naked and were not ashamed.

1 CORINTHIANS 6:15–18

15 Do you not know that your bodies are members of Christ? Shall I then take away the members of Christ and make them members of a prostitute? May it never be!

16 Or do you not know that the one who joins himself to a prostitute is one body with her? For He says, "The two shall become one flesh."

• Discuss how this compares to what you see in our culture today.

OBSERVE

We've seen God's original design for sex between a man and a woman, but did the Designer's intent change with the passing of time or with shifting cultural standards? Let's jump forward several thousand years to the New Testament, where we find Paul writing to the believers in the church at Corinth.

Leader: Read aloud 1 Corinthians 6:15–18 and have the group do the following:
  • *Underline each occurrence of the phrase* **_do you not know._**
  • *Draw a squiggly line under every reference to* **a believer's body,** *including synonyms such as* **members** *and* **himself,** *like this:* ‿‿‿‿
  • *Mark every occurrence of the words* **immorality** *and* **immoral** *with a big* **I.**

DISCUSS

• What did you learn from marking the references to a believer's body in verses 15 and 16? Explain your answer.

• Based on what you have read in this passage and in Genesis 2, how would you explain the meaning of the phrase "the two shall become one flesh"?

• How are believers to respond to immorality, according to verse 18, and why?

OBSERVE

Now that we've confirmed that becoming one flesh refers to being sexually intimate, let's look at another place this phrase is used.

Leader: Read aloud Ephesians 5:25 and 31. Have the group say aloud and…
- *draw a box around the words **husbands, man,** and **his.***
- *circle the words **wives** and **wife.***

17 But the one who joins himself to the Lord is one spirit with Him.

18 Flee immorality. Every other sin that a man commits is outside the body, but the immoral man sins against his own body.

EPHESIANS 5:25, 31

25 Husbands, love your wives, just as Christ also loved the church and gave Himself up for her.…

31 For this reason a man shall leave his father and mother and shall be joined to his wife, and the two shall become one flesh.

DISCUSS

• What did you learn about the "one flesh" relationship in these verses?

• According to this passage, in what circumstances is the sexual relationship to take place?

• From what you have seen so far, what genders were involved in God's original design for both marriage and sexual relationships?

HEBREWS 13:4

Marriage is to be held in honor among all, and the marriage bed is to be undefiled; for fornicators and adulterers God will judge.

OBSERVE

We've seen that God designed sex as a significant part of the marriage relationship, but is sex intended only for people who are married to each other?

Leader: Read Hebrews 13:4.
    • *Have the group say aloud and mark the word* **marriage** *with a big* **M.**

DISCUSS

• What did you learn about God's will for marriage?

• What boundaries have been set for sex, and who established them?

• What right does God have to set the standard for sex?

INSIGHT

The word *fornicator* is translated from the Greek word *pornos,* the root of our English word *pornography.* It refers to any sexual activity outside God's design.

Adulterers refers to individuals participating in any sexual activity where one or both partners are married to someone else.

• What is the consequence of not following God's will when it comes to sex? In other words, if someone who is not married participates in sexual activity, what will God do?

• From all you have seen so far, what effect would fornication and adultery have on marriage?

1 CORINTHIANS 7:1–2, 8–9

¹ Now concerning the things about which you wrote, it is good for a man not to touch a woman.

² But because of immoralities, each man is to have his own wife, and each woman is to have her own husband....

⁸ But I say to the unmarried and to widows that it is good for them if they remain even as I.

⁹ But if they do not have self-control, let them marry; for it is better to marry than to burn with passion.

OBSERVE

The early believers lived in a culture that, much like ours today, treated sex as a cheap thing rather than a unique design of God. In response to questions from the church at Corinth, Paul—an unmarried man himself—wrote the following passage to explain how to deal appropriately with sexual desire.

Leader: *Read 1 Corinthians 7:1–2, 8–9 and have the group...*

- *mark the word **immoralities** with a big* **I.**
- *underline the reference to **self-control.***

INSIGHT

The Greek word translated as *touch* here means "to handle an object to exert an influence over it." It also means "to light a fire." So Paul was referring to any action that ignites sexual passion and desire.

DISCUSS

• According to verses 1 and 2, what is a man to do and why?

• Who is to meet a man's sexual desires? A woman's?

• What was Paul's message to the single and widowed?

• According to verse 9, what is God's solution for dealing with sexual desires?

• From what you have seen so far, and taking into consideration what you read in the Insight box, what did Paul mean when he said, "If they do not have self-control, let them marry"? Was he referring only to sexual intercourse, or was he including other sexual expressions as well? Explain your answer.

• Under what circumstances is sex intended to take place? What purpose(s) is it meant to serve?

WRAP IT UP

Despite what you may have heard, God is not against sex. In fact, from the very beginning He planned for sex to unite a man and his wife. There was no alternate plan, no substitute, and no better companion for man than his wife. God designed the sexual relationship—the union of two into one flesh—to bring the blessings of companionship, unity, and pleasure. God planned on our being sexually satisfied within the marriage relationship.

Sex within the bounds of marriage is awesome; it brings about a dimension of total oneness and completeness that cannot be fully explained to those who haven't experienced it. However, as we'll see in the following weeks, sex outside of marriage violates God's design and can lead to hurt, guilt, shame, and perversion.

God's plan remains unchanged since the beginning of time. No matter how our culture changes and redefines sexual activity, God, the inventor of sex, has clearly set the boundaries for the sexual relationship. Sex is:

designed solely for one man and one woman,
    to be practiced inside marriage only,
        satisfying and pleasurable when enjoyed within God's
        guidelines,
            but dangerous and destructive when practiced
            outside of God's plan.

In a culture saturated with sex and distorted by lust, following God's design may be considered old-fashioned, but it's the only way to enjoy this precious gift without destructive consequences.

Take the time this week to examine yourself and see what ways you may have personally bought into the world's view on sex.

For many people, virginity seems to be a strange idea, quite out of line with our modern-day culture. Any teenager or adult bold enough to admit to remaining a virgin is either looked at as an anomaly or ridiculed outright.

Why should anyone make a big deal about "saving yourself" for marriage? Is it really that important? If so, is it important for both males and females? Isn't it a personal choice whether or not to remain a virgin? Can you still be a virgin if you don't go "all the way"? This week we are going to look at the subject of virginity and find answers to these questions straight from God's Word.

OBSERVE

What value does God place on virginity? As the designer of sex, God created clear boundaries for its use. Let's look at two passages that deal specifically with a woman's virginity prior to marriage.

Leader: *Read Deuteronomy 22:28–29 and Exodus 22:16–17. Have the group say aloud and...*

- *draw a box around every reference to* **the man,** *including pronouns:* ☐
- *mark every reference to* **the virgin** *or* **girl,** *including pronouns, with a big* **V.**

DEUTERONOMY 22:28–29

28 If a man finds a girl who is a virgin, who is not engaged, and seizes her and lies with her and they are discovered,

29 then the man who lay with her shall give to the girl's father fifty shekels of silver, and she shall become his wife because he has violated her; he cannot divorce her all his days.

Exodus 22:16–17

16 If a man seduces a virgin who is not engaged, and lies with her, he must pay a dowry for her to be his wife.

17 If her father absolutely refuses to give her to him, he shall pay money equal to the dowry for virgins.

DISCUSS

• From these verses, what did you learn about man who has sex with or rapes a virgin?

• What exactly is the penalty for his actions?

INSIGHT

The penalty assessed by the law for rape was fifty shekels of silver, the same price as the dowry of a bride. This was a significant fine for violating the law. Combined with the prospect of never being allowed to divorce the girl if her father allowed the marriage, this served as a substantial deterrent to rape and sexual immorality.

How seriously did God view this situation?

OBSERVE

Let's look at another passage that deals with the issue of virginity from a different perspective.

Leader: *Read aloud Deuteronomy 22:13–21 and have the group do the following:*
  - *Mark every occurrence of the words **virgin** or **virginity** with a big **V.***
  - *Draw a box around every reference to **the man,** including pronouns.*
  - *Circle every reference to **the wife,** including pronouns and synonyms such as **woman** and **girl.***

DISCUSS

• Briefly summarize this passage. What sort of accusation was God preparing the Israelites to deal with in these verses?

• What did you learn from marking *virgin*?

DEUTERONOMY 22:13–21

13 If any man takes a wife and goes in to her and then turns against her,

14 and charges her with shameful deeds and publicly defames her, and says, "I took this woman, but when I came near her, I did not find her a virgin,"

15 then the girl's father and her mother shall take and bring out the evidence of the girl's virginity to the elders of the city at the gate.

16 The girl's father shall say to the elders, "I gave my daughter to this man for a wife, but he turned against her;

17 and behold, he has charged her with

shameful deeds, saying, 'I did not find your daughter a virgin.' But this is the evidence of my daughter's virginity." And they shall spread the garment before the elders of the city.

18 So the elders of that city shall take the man and chastise him,

19 and they shall fine him a hundred shekels of silver and give it to the girl's father, because he publicly defamed a virgin of Israel. And she shall remain his wife; he cannot divorce her all his days.

20 But if this charge is true, that the girl was not found a virgin,

INSIGHT

The word *virgin* is used in Scripture only to describe a woman who has not had sexual relations.

The evidence described in verse 15 refers to a bloodstained garment or bed sheet from the wedding night, proof of a ruptured hymen at the woman's first sexual experience. This cloth would be kept as evidence of the bride's virginity. If a man charged that his wife was not a virgin when they married, her parents were obligated to present the proof of her virginity.

• What was the penalty for publicly defaming a virgin in Israel?

• If the charge was true and the girl was found not to be a virgin, what was the consequence?

• Why was this done, according to verse 21?

21 then they shall bring out the girl to the doorway of her father's house, and the men of her city shall stone her to death because she has committed an act of folly in Israel by playing the harlot in her father's house; thus you shall purge the evil from among you.

• In this passage, how much importance is placed on virginity?

OBSERVE

Leader: *Read Deuteronomy 5:18 and Leviticus 20:10.*

> • *Have the group say aloud and mark the words* **adultery, adulterer,** *and* **adulteress** *with a big* **A.**

DEUTERONOMY 5:18

You shall not commit adultery.

LEVITICUS 20:10

If there is a man who commits adultery with another man's wife, one who commits adultery with his friend's wife, the adulterer and the adulteress shall surely be put to death.

DISCUSS

• If the woman mentioned in the Deuteronomy 22 passage was found not to be a virgin, then she would be guilty of adultery. What does God say about adultery?

• What was the punishment for adultery?

• From what you've read in the preceding passages, how seriously does God take virginity?

INSIGHT

Adultery describes any sexual relations between two people where one or both of them is married or engaged to someone else. It refers to a breach of the "one flesh" relationship of marriage.

OBSERVE

Even among those who hold to the ideal of virginity for unmarried women, few seem to have the same standard for men. Let's review the 1 Corinthians passage we looked at last week to see how Paul dealt with this issue within the church. The verses here come from chapter 7 of Paul's first letter to the church in Corinth, Greece, in which he began to answer a series of questions they had posed about the Christian life.

Leader: Read 1 Corinthians 7:1–2, 8–9 and have the group…

- *draw a box around each reference to* **man** *or* **husband***, including pronouns.*
- *circle every reference to* **woman** *or* **wife***, including pronouns.*
- *double underline each reference to* **the unmarried** *or* **widows***, including pronouns.*

INSIGHT

As noted last week, the Greek word translated as *touch* here means "to handle an object to exert an influence over it." It also means "to light a fire." So Paul was referring to any action that ignites sexual passion and desire.

DISCUSS

- What was the Corinthians' concern, according to verse 1?

- Discuss Paul's response to their question and his reasoning.

---

1 CORINTHIANS 7:1–2, 8–9

1 Now concerning the things about which you wrote, it is good for a man not to touch a woman.

2 But because of immoralities, each man is to have his own wife, and each woman is to have her own husband….

8 But I say to the unmarried and to widows that it is good for them if they remain even as I.

9 But if they do not have self-control, let them marry; for it is better to marry than to burn with passion.

• From what you have seen, is it acceptable in God's eyes to engage in premarital sex? Discuss your answer.

• What about those who are single? What are they to do, and why?

• What reason does verse 9 provide for getting married?

• The unmarried in verse 9 would include not only virgins but also divorced persons and those whose spouse had died. Since they had already been sexually active during marriage, is it acceptable for them to continue to be sexually active once the marriage has ended? Explain your answer.

• From what you have seen so far and taking into consideration what you read in the Insight box, what did Paul mean when he said, "if they do not have self-control, let them marry"? Explain your answer.

• According to these verses, is it acceptable for a man to have sex outside of marriage?

• What reasons might your peers give for disregarding God's Word on this subject?

• How would you answer their objections?

• What are some questions or feelings people must deal with when they don't save themselves sexually for their spouses?

2 SAMUEL 13:10–19

10 Then Amnon said to Tamar, "Bring the food into the bedroom, that I may eat from your hand." So Tamar took the cakes which she had made and brought them into the bedroom to her brother Amnon.

11 When she brought them to him to eat, he took hold of her and said to her, "Come, lie with me, my sister."

12 But she answered him, "No, my brother, do not violate me, for such a thing is not done in Israel; do not do this disgraceful thing!

13 "As for me, where could I get rid of my reproach? And as for

OBSERVE

In the Old Testament we find an example of what can happen when someone is controlled by the sexual drive rather than by God's ideal for sex. Amnon was "in love" with Tamar, his stepsister. His cousin Jonadab helped him devise a plan in which Amnon would pretend to be sick and ask his father, David, to allow his sister to take care of him. Then he would compel her to satisfy his sexual appetite as well.

Leader: Read 2 Samuel 13:10–19 aloud. Have the group do the following:
- *Circle every reference to **Tamar**, including pronouns and **my sister**.*
- *Draw a box around every reference to **Amnon**, including pronouns and **my brother**.*
- *Underline each occurrence of the phrase **he would not listen to her**.*

DISCUSS

• Amnon ordered Tamar to bring him food in the privacy of his bedroom. What did he say when she brought it to him?

• How did Tamar respond? What was her first word in response to his request?

• Did Amnon know that what he was asking her to do was wrong? How do you know? Explain your answer.

• What warning did Tamar give about how Amnon's actions would affect both their lives?

• After satisfying his sexual appetite, what feelings did Amnon have toward Tamar? How did he treat her?

you, you will be like one of the fools in Israel. Now therefore, please speak to the king, for he will not withhold me from you."

14 However, he would not listen to her; since he was stronger than she, he violated her and lay with her.

15 Then Amnon hated her with a very great hatred; for the hatred with which he hated her was greater than the love with which he had loved her. And Amnon said to her, "Get up, go away!"

16 But she said to him, "No, because this wrong in sending me away is greater than the other that you have done to me!" Yet he would not listen to her.

17 Then he called his young man who attended him and said, "Now throw this woman out of my presence, and lock the door behind her."

18 Now she had on a long-sleeved garment; for in this manner the virgin daughters of the king dressed themselves in robes. Then his attendant took her out and locked the door behind her.

19 Tamar put ashes on her head and tore her long-sleeved garment which was on her; and she put her hand on her head and went away, crying aloud as she went.

• What does this tell you about his original feelings for her? Was he really in love? Explain your answer.

• According to verse 16, what did Tamar say to Amnon and how did he respond? How does this compare to what you saw in Deuteronomy 22:29 at the start of this lesson?

• What was Tamar's response to the loss of her virginity? Discuss the scene in verses 17–19.

INSIGHT

Amnon was later murdered by another brother, Absalom, for his cruel violation of Tamar.

OBSERVE

Although we have already looked at the following passages, it won't hurt to consider them again and be reminded of God's original design for the sexual relationship. Even though the culture changes, God's moral code never alters.

Leader: Read aloud Genesis 2:22–25 and Hebrews 13:4. Have the group do the following:

- *Draw a box around every reference to **man**, including pronouns.*
- *Circle every reference to **woman** and **wife**, including pronouns.*
- *Underline the phrase **they shall become one flesh.***
- *Mark the word **marriage** with a big **M**.*

DISCUSS

- For whom was sex intended, in God's original design? Explain your answer.

GENESIS 2:22–25

22 The LORD God fashioned into a woman the rib which He had taken from the man, and brought her to the man.

23 The man said, "This is now bone of my bones, and flesh of my flesh; she shall be called Woman, because she was taken out of Man."

24 For this reason a man shall leave his father and his mother, and be joined to his wife; and they shall become one flesh.

25 And the man and his wife were both naked and were not ashamed.

HEBREWS 13:4

Marriage is to be held in honor among all, and the marriage bed is to be undefiled; for fornicators and adulterers God will judge.

INSIGHT

Fornication is defined as any kind of sexual relations that violate God's design. That is, any sexual experiences except those between a husband and wife. It includes, but is not limited to, sexual activity between unmarried persons, such as homosexuality, lesbianism, oral sex, heavy petting, and inappropriate touching.

Adultery describes any sexual relations between two people where one or both of them is married or engaged to someone else.

• What did you learn about marriage from Hebrews 13:4?

• How will God deal with fornicators and adulterers?

WRAP IT UP

You have seen it in the Word of God for yourself: regardless of what the culture says or what temptation comes, both men and women are to remain virgins until marriage.

Today many have bought into the lie that as long as they don't "go all the way" everything else is allowed—oral sex, heavy petting, inappropriate touching, nudity, and more. But as you have clearly seen in the Bible this week, there is no place for any sexual behavior or touch outside of marriage.

Sadly, too many young people mistakenly believe that sex is all about the physical act, and they ignore the dangerous consequences of abusing this priceless gift. Like Amnon, men—and these days, women as well—devise schemes to satisfy their sexual appetites. They proclaim their love and continually push and pressure until the other person believes that giving in to sex is the only way to continue the relationship.

By contrast, genuine love demonstrates gentleness and consideration, however strong the sexual desire may be. First Corinthians 13 gives us a clear portrait of how genuine love shows itself. Comparing your treatment of others—and their treatment of you—against this standard provides powerful protection against cultural and peer pressure.

God never has a double standard. If you follow the Designer's directions and refuse to compromise the purity and sanctity of sex, you will know the joy that comes to those who trust Him to have their best interests at heart.

How would you counsel the unmarried regarding their dating relationships? Whether you are single or married, what are you doing to guard yourself against the temptation to satisfy your sexual desires outside of marriage?

Our responsibility before God is to be holy, which means we are to stand apart from the world and the culture of the day. Our lives are to be different in all aspects, including our sexuality. This week we will begin to look at God's guidelines regarding our sexuality, in order to practice them and be pleasing to Him.

OBSERVE

The book of Leviticus records God speaking to the children of Israel through Moses. At the end of chapter 11 Moses reminded them of the purpose behind God's laws, a purpose repeatedly declared throughout the book of Leviticus.

Leader: Read Leviticus 11:45 and 20:7–8 aloud. Have the group say aloud and...
- *mark each occurrence of the word **holy** with an arrow, like this:* ↑
- *draw a cloud like this* ☁ *around each occurrence of the phrase **I am the Lord.***

DISCUSS

- What did you learn from marking *holy* in these verses?

LEVITICUS 11:45

"For I am the LORD who brought you up from the land of Egypt to be your God; thus you shall be holy, for I am holy."

LEVITICUS 20:7–8

7 "You shall consecrate yourselves therefore and be holy, for I am the LORD your God.

8 "You shall keep My statutes and practice them; I am the LORD who sanctifies you."

• What, specifically, were the Israelites instructed to do in Leviticus 11:45?

• Why were they to do this?

INSIGHT

The word *holy* means "to be dedicated." Anything holy is set apart for God's purposes. Because God is holy, those associated with Him are to be holy in all they do, including their sexual behavior.

• According to Leviticus 20:8, how are the people of Israel to achieve this?

OBSERVE

Leviticus records Moses telling the children of Israel about the boundaries God has set for their good and for the nation's holiness. Let's look at a portion of chapter 18, which defines some specific boundaries for the family.

Leader: Read Leviticus 18:3–5 and have group do the following:

- *Mark each occurrence of the word* **you,** *which in this passage refers to* **the people of Israel,** *like this:* ✡

- *Mark every reference to* **God,** *including the pronouns* **I** *and* **My** *and the synonym* **the Lord,** *with a triangle, like this:* △

- *Draw a cloud around each occurrence of the phrase* **I am the Lord.**

INSIGHT

Among the Egyptians, sex was a family affair; pharaohs often married their close relatives. The Canaanites held an "anything goes" philosophy about sex. They participated in sex among family members, sex with the same sex, sex with animals. Sex was also involved in the worship of their gods, as their religious mythology was filled with perversion and promiscuity.

LEVITICUS 18:3–5

3 "You shall not do what is done in the land of Egypt where you lived, nor are you to do what is done in the land of Canaan where I am bringing you; you shall not walk in their statutes.

4 "You are to perform My judgments and keep My statutes, to live in accord with them; I am the LORD your God.

5 "So you shall keep My statutes and My judgments, by which a man may live if he does them; I am the LORD."

DISCUSS

• What instructions did God give to the children of Israel in these verses?

• Why do you think God said, "I am the LORD your God" in this passage? What point was He making?

• What would be the results of following God's statutes and judgments?

---

1 PETER 1:14–16

14 As obedient children, do not be conformed to the former lusts which were yours in your ignorance,

15 but like the Holy One who called you, be holy yourselves also in all your behavior;

OBSERVE

Let's look at a New Testament passage that shows whether or not holiness is solely an Old Testament principle.

Leader: Read 1 Peter 1:14–16 aloud. Have the group...

> • *draw a triangle over every reference to **God**, including the pronoun **I** and the synonym **the Holy One.***
> • *mark each occurrence of the word **holy** with an arrow:* ↑

DISCUSS

• As a believer, how will you benefit from walking in obedience to God's Word in regard to your sexuality? What would it look like for you to live a separate or holy life?

• Can you expect the world to understand? Explain your answer.

• One of the most common excuses for sexual promiscuity we hear today is "everybody's doing it." The idea is that anything so widespread must be okay. Many students are ridiculed in high school and even middle school now for being virgins. Adults who are single or "single again" particularly feel the pressures of our culture as they're led to believe that sexual promiscuity is normal. From all we have seen, is the excuse "everybody's doing it" any more valid today than it was in the days of the Israelites? Explain your answer.

16 because it is written, "You shall be holy, for I am holy."

LEVITICUS 18:6–18

6 "None of you shall approach any blood relative of his to uncover nakedness; I am the LORD.

7 "You shall not uncover the nakedness of your father, that is, the nakedness of your mother. She is your mother; you are not to uncover her nakedness.

8 "You shall not uncover the nakedness of your father's wife; it is your father's nakedness.

9 "The nakedness of your sister, either your father's daughter or your mother's daughter, whether born at home or born outside, their nakedness you shall not uncover.

OBSERVE

Since God invented sex and ordained marriage, as we saw in lesson one, He has the right to establish rules to protect them.

Let's continue in our study of Leviticus 18 and see some of God's rules for sexual activity within the family. We realize many of the situations described in this passage sound bizarre and even gross. But we need to know what God says on this topic and consider its relevance for preserving the sanctity of the family in our current society.

Leader: Read Leviticus 18:6–18 aloud. Have the group say aloud and...

- *underline each occurrence of the command* **you shall not uncover the nakedness of** *and related phrases.*
- *mark multiple slashes through each occurrence of the phrase* **blood relative,** *like this: ///*
- *draw a cloud like this* ⛅ *around each occurrence of the phrase* **I am the Lord.**

INSIGHT

To *uncover the nakedness of* is another way of saying *to have sexual relations with*. It is an important phrase in defining incest.

DISCUSS

• Twelve types of incestuous relationships are described here, and the principles outlined prohibit both casual sexual intercourse and marriage in these relationships. Go through the verses and make a list of relationships in which sex was prohibited for the children of Israel, noting what God says about each situation.

10 "The nakedness of your son's daughter or your daughter's daughter, their nakedness you shall not uncover; for their nakedness is yours.

11 "The nakedness of your father's wife's daughter, born to your father, she is your sister, you shall not uncover her nakedness.

12 "You shall not uncover the nakedness of your father's sister; she is your father's blood relative.

13 "You shall not uncover the nakedness of your mother's sister, for she is your mother's blood relative.

14 "You shall not uncover the nakedness

of your father's brother; you shall not approach his wife, she is your aunt.

15 "You shall not uncover the nakedness of your daughter-in-law; she is your son's wife, you shall not uncover her nakedness.

16 "You shall not uncover the nakedness of your brother's wife; it is your brother's nakedness.

17 "You shall not uncover the nakedness of a woman and of her daughter, nor shall you take her son's daughter or her daughter's daughter, to uncover her nakedness; they are blood relatives. It is lewdness.

• Who would be included under the category "blood relatives"? Who would not be included?

• God was very specific in His instructions. Would there have been any doubt or uncertainty in the minds of the children of Israel about who and what He was talking about? Why do you think God outlined His instructions so specifically?

• Several times we see the uncovering of the wife's nakedness equated with the husband's nakedness. Discuss how this relates to what you learned from Genesis 2:24 in lesson one.

• Again we see the phrase "I am the LORD." What point do you think He was making?

• How would the breaking of these laws affect the family? The culture? The church?

• Discuss what you see in our culture today as a result of the boundaries for sex being blurred.

OBSERVE

Let's move ahead to Leviticus 20, where we find the consequences of violating the boundaries God has set.

Leader: Read aloud the verses printed out on this page and have the group...
   • *draw a box around every reference to* **man,** *including pronouns.*
   • *underline each reference to* **sexual relations,** *including synonyms such as* **lies with, uncovered...nakedness,** *and* **takes.**

18 "You shall not marry a woman in addition to her sister as a rival while she is alive, to uncover her nakedness."

LEVITICUS 20:11–12, 17, 19–21

11 "If there is a man who lies with his father's wife, he has uncovered his father's nakedness; both of them shall surely be put to death, their blood-guiltiness is upon them.

12 "If there is a man who lies with his daughter-in-law, both of them shall surely be put to death; they have committed incest, their bloodguiltiness is upon them....

17 "If there is a man who takes his sister, his father's daughter or his mother's daughter, so that he sees her nakedness and she sees his nakedness, it is a disgrace; and they shall be cut off in the sight of the sons of their people. He has uncovered his sister's nakedness; he bears his guilt....

19 "You shall also not uncover the nakedness of your mother's sister or of your father's sister, for such a one has made naked his blood relative; they will bear their guilt.

20 "If there is a man who lies with his uncle's wife he has uncovered his uncle's

DISCUSS

• List the punishment for each scenario described in these verses.

• How serious is this kind of sin to God and why? Explain your answer.

OBSERVE

Let's look at a portion of Scripture in which God instructed the leaders of Israel to declare before the people some specific behaviors that would bring a curse upon the offender.

Leader: Read Deuteronomy 27:20, 22–23.
  • *Have the group say aloud and underline each occurrence of the phrase **cursed is he who lies with**.*

DISCUSS

• Who was cursed and why, according to these verses?

nakedness; they will bear their sin. They will die childless.

21 "If there is a man who takes his brother's wife, it is abhorrent; he has uncovered his brother's nakedness. They will be childless."

DEUTERONOMY 27:20, 22–23

20 "Cursed is he who lies with his father's wife, because he has uncovered his father's skirt." And all the people shall say, "Amen."…

22 "Cursed is he who lies with his sister, the daughter of his father or of his mother." And all the people shall say, "Amen."

23 "Cursed is he who lies with his mother-in-law." And all the people shall say, "Amen."

• How were the people to respond to God's declaration? What does it mean?

INSIGHT

The word *amen* is a Hebrew word that could be translated as *so be it* or *may it be so* or *very true*. It indicates a strong affirmation of what was just said.

ROMANS 15:4

For whatever was written in earlier times was written for our instruction, so that through perseverance and the encouragement of the Scriptures we might have hope.

OBSERVE

You may have noticed that many of the passages we've examined this week are from the Old Testament. Do they apply to Christians today as well as to the people of Israel?

Let's look at a couple of New Testament passages to find out.

Leader: *Read Romans 15:4 aloud.*

> • *Have the group say aloud and mark the word **written** with a squiggly line, like this:* ∿∿∿∿

DISCUSS

• The things written in earlier times were written for what purpose?

• What result do they bring to our lives?

From what you have seen, would the passages we studied in this lesson from Leviticus and Deuteronomy apply to us today? Explain your answer.

OBSERVE

At first all the members of the early church were Jewish. When Gentiles, or non-Jews, started becoming Christ followers, the coming together of different cultures created a crisis. The church leaders were uncertain about which parts of the Old Testament law applied to Gentile believers. Let's see what they decided. By the way, the Simeon mentioned in verse 14 is the apostle Peter, who had walked with Jesus as one of His Jewish disciples.

Acts 15:12–14, 19–20

12 All the people kept silent, and they were listening to Barnabas and Paul as they were relating what signs and wonders God had done through them among the Gentiles.

13 After they had stopped speaking,

James answered, say-
ing, "Brethren, listen
to me.

14 "Simeon has
related how God first
concerned Himself
about taking from
among the Gentiles a
people for His
name....

19 "Therefore it is my
judgment that we do
not trouble those who
are turning to God
from among the
Gentiles,

20 but that we write
to them that they
abstain from things
contaminated by idols
and from fornication
and from what is
strangled and from
blood."

Leader: *Read Acts 15:12–14 and 19–20*
aloud.

> • *Have the group say aloud and draw a*
> *box around each reference to* **the Gen-**
> **tiles,** *including pronouns.*

DISCUSS

• What did church leaders decide to require
of the Gentiles?

• Would these same things apply to us today? Explain your answer.

WRAP IT UP

Although we saw it only three times, the phrase *I am the* LORD appears six times in Leviticus 18. God was establishing His authority as well as the responsibility of His covenant people to obey His commandments.

Years before, God had promised to create a great nation through Abraham's descendants. This family, later known as Israel, was to be a peculiar people, set apart for His purposes. But if the family unit was undermined, the nation could not flourish, for the family is the foundation of any society. God intended the family to be a network characterized by honor, respect, and proper behavior toward one another, not destroyed by abuse. Incest blurs family lines, leading to the destruction of the family unit and the nation. So as the people of Israel grew into a nation, God defined acceptable sexual relationships and set boundaries for their protection.

God warned Israel not to look back and imitate what they had seen in Egypt. They also were not to follow the ways of other nations. When they entered the Promised Land they would find the Canaanites to be horribly immoral, and they would have to keep themselves separated in order to be pleasing to God.

We must do the same today. As we saw in Romans 15:4, these things were written for our instruction today as well as in Old Testament times; God's plan for the family to serve as a place of safety and respect has not changed. Most of us realize incest is wrong, yet it is frighteningly prevalent in our culture. If you have been a victim of incest, we want you to know that what happened to you is wrong and it is not your fault. God will deal with the one that abused you.[1]

We are created in the image of God, and the Creator knows what is best for His creation. Since God invented sex and ordained marriage, He has the right to establish the rules governing them. He wants married couples to enjoy the gift of sex, but He wants to protect all of His people from the consequences that come from violating His laws.

---

[1] If you or someone you know has been a victim of incest, we recommend *Lord, Heal My Heart* by Kay Arthur.

As Christians, our marriages should serve as an illustration of the love Christ has for the church. However, if a marriage isn't everything it should be, then the witness is worthless.

As we've seen, God designed sex as an expression of intimate love between a *husband* and *wife*. However, in the media and throughout our culture we are bombarded with the message that monogamy is outdated and anything is acceptable between two consenting adults.

This week we'll look at what God says about sex outside of marriage and learn whether such behavior is as harmless as many believe.

OBSERVE

Let's first look briefly at a few Old Testament verses that reveal God's view on sexual intimacy outside of marriage.

Leader: *Read the following verses aloud.*
   • *Have the group mark the words* **adultery** *and* **intercourse** *with a big* **A.**

DISCUSS

• What did you learn from marking *adultery* in these verses?

EXODUS 20:14

You shall not commit adultery.

LEVITICUS 18:20

You shall not have intercourse with your neighbor's wife, to be defiled with her.

LEVITICUS 20:10

If there is a man who commits adultery with another man's wife, one who commits adultery with his friend's wife, the adulterer and the adulteress shall surely be put to death.

INSIGHT

Adultery refers to sexual intercourse between a married person and someone other than his or her spouse. In the Bible it would also include sex with someone else's fiancé. Adultery ruptures the "one flesh" relationship of marriage.

• What consequence is specified for adultery in Leviticus 20:10?

• How has adultery affected today's families and ultimately our culture?

DEUTERONOMY 22:22–27

22 If a man is found lying with a married woman, then both of them shall die, the man who lay with the woman, and the woman; thus you shall purge the evil from Israel.

OBSERVE

Deuteronomy is a book of the Law, detailing how Israel was to be ruled by God and His laws, statutes, and judgments. This portion of the Law deals with sexual crimes and immorality, providing very specific instructions so that Israel would know exactly how to handle every situation.

Leader: *Read Deuteronomy 22:22–27.*
Have the group say aloud and...
- *underline the phrases **lying with, lay with,** and **lies with.***
- *mark each occurrence of the words **die** and **death** with a tombstone, like this:*

$\cap$

DISCUSS

- These verses outline the consequences for three different scenarios. Look at each one separately and summarize the situation, the persons involved, the consequence, and the reason given.

verse 22

verses 23–24

verses 25–27

- In each case who was held accountable for the sin?

- Why?

23 If there is a girl who is a virgin engaged to a man, and another man finds her in the city and lies with her,

24 then you shall bring them both out to the gate of that city and you shall stone them to death; the girl, because she did not cry out in the city, and the man, because he has violated his neighbor's wife. Thus you shall purge the evil from among you.

25 But if in the field the man finds the girl who is engaged, and the man forces her and lies with her, then only the man who lies with her shall die.

26 But you shall do nothing to the girl; there is no sin in the girl worthy of death, for just as a man rises against his neighbor and murders him, so is this case.

27 When he found her in the field, the engaged girl cried out, but there was no one to save her.

INSIGHT

A *covenant* is a formal, solemn binding agreement between two parties. A marriage is a covenant. In the wedding, promises or vows are made between the bride and groom in the presence of witnesses and God Himself. God takes covenants and our promises very seriously. He keeps His promises and expects us to do the same.

• We saw in an earlier lesson that, according to Hebrews 13:4, the covenant relationship of marriage is to be honored and the marriage bed is to be undefiled. Can a covenant be broken without consequences?

• What is the evil that is to be purged, gotten rid of? Discuss why this behavior is such a big deal to God and why He calls it evil.

• People are not stoned anymore, but God still judges sin. Discuss the difference it would make in our lives if we really understood the judgment that always follows the flagrant disobedience of God's commands, even for believers.

OBSERVE

Proverbs 5 deals with the wisdom of not being involved in adultery. With that in mind let's see what God has to say.

Leader: Read Proverbs 5:15–23 aloud. Have the group…
- *draw a squiggly line under every occurrence of the words **you, your,** and **yours,** like this* 〰〰〰
- *draw a box around the word **man** and the pronouns referring to him.*

DISCUSS

• Keeping in mind the context of Proverbs 5—the wisdom of not being involved in adultery—what do you believe the father is warning his son about in verses 15 and 16?

PROVERBS 5:15–23

15 Drink water from your own cistern and fresh water from your own well.

16 Should your springs be dispersed abroad, streams of water in the streets?

17 Let them be yours alone and not for strangers with you.

18 Let your fountain be blessed, and rejoice in the wife of your youth.

19 As a loving hind and a graceful doe, let her breasts satisfy you at all times; be exhilarated always with her love.

20 For why should you, my son, be exhilarated with an adulteress and embrace the bosom of a foreigner?

21 For the ways of a man are before the eyes of the LORD, and He watches all his paths.

22 His own iniquities will capture the wicked, and he will be held with the cords of his sin.

23 He will die for lack of instruction, and in the greatness of his folly he will go astray.

• The author of Proverbs 5 seems to be encouraging sex in verses 18 and 19. Who is to be the object of a man's sexual attention?

• Even if no one else knows what is going on, who will know the adulterer's secret?

• What consequences does God promise to the man who has an affair?

• God created sex not just for reproduction but also for enjoyment. From what you have seen, how does the outcome of sex within marriage (verses 18–19) contrast with the outcome of adultery?

OBSERVE

In the Sermon on the Mount in Matthew 5–7, Jesus defined the intent of the Old Testament law and how it applies to His followers.

Leader: Read aloud Matthew 5:27–30.
   • *Have the group say aloud and mark each occurrence of the word **adultery** with a big* **A.**

DISCUSS

• What point was Jesus making in this passage?

• According to Jesus, where does adultery begin? Discuss what difference this knowledge should make in a person's response to temptation.

• With that in mind, what place do sexual images—whether in pornography, Internet sites, magazines, movies, etc.—have in a believer's life?

MATTHEW 5:27–30

27 "You have heard that it was said, 'You shall not commit adultery';

28 "but I say to you that everyone who looks at a woman with lust for her has already committed adultery with her in his heart.

29 "If your right eye makes you stumble, tear it out and throw it from you; for it is better for you to lose one of the parts of your body, than for your whole body to be thrown into hell.

30 "If your right hand makes you stumble, cut it off and throw it from you; for it is better for you to lose one

of the parts of your body, than for your whole body to go into hell."

ROMANS 13:8–10

8 Owe nothing to anyone except to love one another; for he who loves his neighbor has fulfilled the law.

9 For this, "You shall not commit adultery, you shall not murder, you shall not steal, you shall not covet," and if there is any other commandment, it is summed up in this saying, "You shall love your neighbor as yourself."

10 Love does no wrong to a neighbor; therefore love is the fulfillment of the law.

• Was Jesus really advocating self-mutilation? Would being blind or disabled protect a person from sexual temptations? What was His point? Explain your answer.

OBSERVE

Paul, in his letter to the church in Rome, provided further insight into how we should and should not respond to each other as believers.

Leader: Read Romans 13:8–10 aloud. Have the group say aloud and…
- *draw a heart over every reference to* **love:** ♡
- *mark the word* **adultery** *with a big* **A.**

DISCUSS

• What did you learn from marking *love* in this passage?

• Discuss how love relates to adultery.

• Who might be considered a neighbor in this context?

WRAP IT UP

Marriage is a covenant, a commitment of mutual loyalty and fidelity. It is meant to be a picture of God's relationship with His people. Sex is intended to bind two people together in the most intimate of human relationships. Within the context of the marriage covenant, sex is beautiful and right. In any other context it is destructive and wrong.

God forbids adultery because, among other things, it ruptures the "one flesh" relationship, causing grief and anguish.

As Christians we are not to practice the sins of those around us even if they are socially acceptable. We are to be radically different! That is one of the hallmarks of a believer. We need to remember that we are to glorify God in everything we do. Our behavior should always encourage and strengthen those around us.

Because we have been called to love God and love people, we must commit both to honoring our own marriages and to helping others do the same.

In the past few weeks we've looked at God's design for sex, including the limits He set for its proper use. We've seen that any sexual behavior outside the bonds of the marriage covenant is damaging to the people involved as well as to their families and to society.

We've looked already at the problem of adultery, something our culture condones but which God condemns because He knows its destructive effects. This week we will examine some other areas of sexual activity in which many today advocate tolerance and acceptance, particularly the topic of homosexuality. Same-sex relationships receive a great deal of attention in our nation today as gay men and lesbians demand not just civil rights but full acceptance of their "alternative lifestyle." Some states are legalizing gay marriages as well as gay adoptions. Even some church groups are ordaining homosexuals as well as allowing homosexuality to be practiced openly among their members.

Is homosexuality an acceptable expression of love between two people or a violation of God's design? As difficult as this subject is to discuss, God's Word is clear. Let's find out what He says.

OBSERVE

Homosexuality was associated with pagan worship in Egypt, Canaan, and other places in the ancient world. Remember, God's command to His people was to "be holy, for I am holy" (Leviticus 11:45).

LEVITICUS 18:22

You shall not lie with a male as one lies with a female; it is an abomination.

LEVITICUS 20:13

If there is a man who lies with a male as those who lie with a woman, both of them have committed a detestable act; they shall surely be put to death. Their blood-guiltiness is upon them.

Leader: *Read aloud Leviticus 18:22 and 20:13.*

> • *Have the group say aloud and underline the words **lies** and **lie**.*

INSIGHT

Detestable is a word used in the Old Testament to express strong revulsion. It describes practices that are morally disgusting to God.

Abomination is another way to say "disgusting, despicable, or repulsive." It is often used of idolatry, the worship of something other than the one, true God, as well as homosexuality.

DISCUSS

• What sexual activity is described in these verses?

• What words are used to describe this behavior? Based on what you read in the Insight box, how strongly does God feel about this?

• What consequence did God specify for this behavior, and why? Explain your answer.

• Keeping in mind that God's people are called to holiness, discuss how God's name is affected when His people participate in such activities.

OBSERVE

Did God's position on homosexual behavior change with the passing of time? Let's find out the answer as we read what Paul said on this issue to the church in Rome when he wrote about those who decided to ignore God's design for sex. Note particularly God's response to their behavior.

Leader: *Read Romans 1:24–27. Have the group say aloud and…*

- *circle the pronouns* **them** *and* **their,** *which refer the* **Romans.**
- *underline the phrase* **God gave them over.**

24 Therefore God gave them over in the lusts of their hearts to impurity, so that their bodies would be dishonored among them.

25 For they exchanged the truth of God for a lie, and worshiped and served the creature rather than the Creator, who is blessed forever. Amen.

26 For this reason God gave them over to degrading passions; for their women exchanged the natural function for that which is unnatural,

27 and in the same way also the men abandoned the natural function of the woman and burned in their desire toward one another, men with men committing indecent acts and receiving in their own persons the due penalty of their error.

DISCUSS

• What did you learn about the Romans being discussed in this passage?

• According to verse 25, what had they done that prompted God to take action?

• What lie had they embraced?

• What did God give them "over to," and why?

• What is described as natural in this passage? Unnatural? Discuss how you see the truth of these verses manifested today.

OBSERVE

The city of Corinth was steeped in immorality. Its religious activity centered on the goddess Aphrodite and involved prostitution and orgies. The believers in this city had been rescued from sin, but some were tempted to go back. Paul, knowing this, had strong words for the church in Corinth.

Leader: *Read 1 Corinthians 6:9–11. Have the group say aloud and...*
- *draw a slash through the word **unrighteous**, like this:*
- *mark the word **homosexuals** with a big* **H.**

INSIGHT

The Greek word translated *effeminate* in verse 9 is *malakoi,* and it is used to describe a passive partner in a homosexual relationship.

---

1 CORINTHIANS 6:9–11

9 Or do you not know that the unrighteous will not inherit the kingdom of God? Do not be deceived; neither fornicators, nor idolaters, nor adulterers, nor effeminate, nor homosexuals,

10 nor thieves, nor the covetous, nor drunkards, nor revilers, nor swindlers, will inherit the kingdom of God.

11 Such were some of you; but you were washed, but you were sanctified, but you were justified in the name of the Lord Jesus Christ and in the Spirit of our God.

DISCUSS

• What did you learn about the unrighteous?

• According to this passage, what are some
of the characteristics of the unrighteous?
How does homosexuality fit into the
picture?

• Discuss what you learned in verse 11 and
how it relates to homosexual behavior
among believers.

• After we become Christians, we still are
capable of sin, but such behavior results
from isolated choices rather than an
ongoing lifestyle. What warning is given
in verse 9, and what does it imply?

OBSERVE

The letter we call Ephesians was written by
the apostle Paul to the young church in
Ephesus, instructing them in the change
their faith should make in their lifestyle.

Leader: *Read Ephesians 5:3–6. Have the group...*

- *mark the words **immorality, immoral, impurity,** and **impure** with a big **I**.*
- *underline the phrase <u>**let no one deceive you.**</u>*

DISCUSS

- What did you learn about immorality and impurity in this passage?

- As we've seen, *immorality* includes any sexual behavior outside of marriage between a man and a woman. With that in mind, what does this passage indicate about a believer's involvement with homosexuality? Explain your answer.

- What warning did you find in verse 6?

EPHESIANS 5:3–6

3 But immorality or any impurity or greed must not even be named among you, as is proper among saints;

4 and there must be no filthiness and silly talk, or coarse jesting, which are not fitting, but rather giving of thanks.

5 For this you know with certainty, that no immoral or impure person or covetous man, who is an idolater, has an inheritance in the kingdom of Christ and God.

6 Let no one deceive you with empty words, for because of these things the wrath of God comes upon the sons of disobedience.

GALATIANS 5:19–21

¹⁹ Now the deeds of the flesh are evident, which are: immorality, impurity, sensuality,

²⁰ idolatry, sorcery, enmities, strife, jealousy, outbursts of anger, disputes, dissensions, factions,

²¹ envying, drunkenness, carousing, and things like these, of which I forewarn you, just as I have forewarned you, that those who practice such things will not inherit the kingdom of God.

OBSERVE

The following passage comes just after Paul urged the Galatian believers to walk in the Spirit and not according to the flesh. In the verses we'll examine here, he identified some actions clearly opposed to the Spirit that lives within believers.

Leader: Read Galatians 5:19–21.

> • *Have the group say and mark the words* **immorality** *and* **impurity** *with an* **I.**

DISCUSS

• What did you learn about immorality and impurity from this passage?

• According to what we see in verse 21, what can we know is true of a person who practices these things as a habitual lifestyle?

• From all you have seen in the Scriptures, is homosexuality or lesbianism a viable alternative lifestyle for a believer? Discuss your answer.

OBSERVE

Both the Canaanites and the Egyptians practiced bestiality—having sex with animals—as a part of their idolatrous worship. Although it sounds bizarre to most of us, it is still a behavior practiced today. References to bestiality abound on the Internet, with Google showing over three million hits, so we can't pretend it is not an issue. God addressed it, and we need to know what He says on the subject.

Leader: Read Exodus 22:19, Leviticus 20:15–16, and Deuteronomy 27:21.
  • *Have the group underline the phrases* **lies with an animal** *and* **approaches any animal to mate with it.**

DISCUSS

• What did you learn from these verses?

• How seriously does God view this offense? What consequence was to be administered? Explain your answer.

EXODUS 22:19

Whoever lies with an animal shall surely be put to death.

LEVITICUS 20:15–16

15 If there is a man who lies with an animal, he shall surely be put to death; you shall also kill the animal.

16 If there is a woman who approaches any animal to mate with it, you shall kill the woman and the animal; they shall surely be put to death. Their blood-guiltiness is upon them.

DEUTERONOMY 27:21

"Cursed is he who lies with any animal." And all the people shall say, "Amen."

• According to Deuteronomy 27:21, what is the fate of the person who participates in such evil?

• How were the people to respond? Remember we learned the word *amen* means "may it be so." What are the people signifying by responding in this way?

LEVITICUS 18:24–30

24 "Do not defile yourselves by any of these things; for by all these the nations which I [God] am casting out before you have become defiled.

OBSERVE

Sexual perversion is like a disease, and that disease can make a society sick. God has a special relationship with the nation of Israel, so you expect His laws to apply to them. Do God's moral laws apply to everyone else as well?

Leader: Read Leviticus 18:24–30. Have the group…

- *mark the words **defile** and **defiled** with a big **X**.*
- *draw a squiggly line under each occurrence of the words **abominations** and **abominable**:* 〰〰〰

As you read through this passage, keep in mind the context. The theme for the book of Leviticus is holiness. "These things" in verse 24 refers to the sexual sins named earlier in the chapter.

DISCUSS

- Discuss the warning given to the Israelites in verses 24–25. What was it and why was it given?

25 "For the land has become defiled, therefore I have brought its punishment upon it, so the land has spewed out its inhabitants.

26 "But as for you, you are to keep My statutes and My judgments and shall not do any of these abominations, neither the native, nor the alien who sojourns among you

27 "(for the men of the land who have been before you have done all these abominations, and the land has become defiled);

28 "so that the land will not spew you out, should you defile it, as it has spewed out the nation which has been before you.

29 "For whoever does any of these abominations, those persons who do so shall be cut off from among their people.

30 "Thus you are to keep My charge, that you do not practice any of the abominable customs which have been practiced before you, so as not to defile yourselves with them; I am the LORD your God."

• Thinking back to all we have seen these past few weeks, specifically what would cause the nation to become defiled?

• According to verse 24, why did God cast out the nations from their land?

• Not only had the nations become defiled, what else had become defiled, according to verse 25?

- What instruction was given to the Israelites in verse 26? Who else was expected to obey this instruction?

- If the Israelites did not follow God's instruction but became like the other nations, what could they expect? Explain your answer.

- According to verse 30 what warning was given specifically to the Israelites, and why?

- We saw God emphasizing His authority in the lives of the Israelites. What kind of authority does He have in the lives of believers? Think about it.

WRAP IT UP

Today, simply calling homosexuality sin can get a person sued or even arrested for a hate crime. Many even claim that the Bible doesn't specifically address the issue, let alone condemn homosexual behavior. But as we've seen, both Exodus and Leviticus identify such behavior as a sin—a sin serious enough to incur the death penalty under the Old Testament law. In the New Testament as well Paul identified homosexual acts among believers as something that "dishonored" their bodies and he spoke of the degrading passions that lead to such "indecent acts" (Romans 1:24–27). Whatever the culture says about homosexuality, the Bible clearly identifies this sexual practice as sin.

Still, as Christians we can take a moral stand on what is right without name-calling or other hurtful behaviors. We must speak the truth in love, carefully choosing our words to those outside the church to emphasize the forgiveness for all sins that comes with personal faith in Jesus Christ.

However, those who claim to be Christians and yet practice homosexuality—or any behavior outside the boundaries God has set—must be challenged with the truth of our holy God, who insists that all who have a relationship with Him depart from their iniquity to live a holy and godly life. In this, as in all areas of life, we are to be holy as He is holy.

We have clearly seen that God desires His people to be unique, separate from the world. But what if you have already messed up? Is it possible to be in a right relationship with God after you have violated His laws? What can you do to heal from the past?

These are the questions we'll look at in our final week.

OBSERVE

Is forgiveness possible for those who repent, who change their mind about their actions and turn away from them? Let's look again at the apostle Paul's reminder to the Christ followers in Corinth.

Leader: *Read 1 Corinthians 6:9–11 aloud. Have the group say and…*

- *circle the phrase* **such were some of you.**
- *underline the phrase* **but you were.**

DISCUSS

• According to what you read in this passage, who will not inherit the kingdom of God?

1 CORINTHIANS 6:9–11

⁹ Do you not know that the unrighteous will not inherit the kingdom of God? Do not be deceived; neither fornicators, nor idolaters, nor adulterers, nor effeminate, nor homosexuals,

¹⁰ nor thieves, nor the covetous, nor drunkards, nor revilers, nor swindlers, will inherit the kingdom of God.

¹¹ Such were some of you; but you were washed, but you were

sanctified, but you were justified in the name of the Lord Jesus Christ and in the Spirit of our God.

• Of the characteristics listed, which ones particularly relate to what we have studied the past several weeks?

INSIGHT

Washed means "to be cleansed, to be free from sin."

Sanctified means "to make clean, to make pure; to set aside as holy."

Justified means "to be made righteous or godly."

• What was Paul reminding the Corinthians about in these verses?

• How were they washed and cleansed of their sins and made new?

OBSERVE

Let's continue on in 1 Corinthians 6 to see what else Paul wanted the early believers to know about living in the light of their new life in Christ.

Leader: Read 1 Corinthians 6:15–20 aloud. Have the group say and…

- *draw a squiggly line under the words **bodies** and **members:*** 〰〰〰
- *mark the word **immorality** with a big* **I.**

DISCUSS

- Because of all God had done for these believers, what responsibility did they bear for the use of their bodies?

15 Do you not know that your bodies are members of Christ? Shall I then take away the members of Christ and make them members of a prostitute? May it never be!

16 Or do you not know that the one who joins himself to a prostitute is one body with her? For He says, "The two shall become one flesh."

17 But the one who joins himself to the Lord is one spirit with Him.

18 Flee immorality. Every other sin that a man commits is outside the body, but the immoral man sins against his own body.

19 Or do you not know that your body is a temple of the Holy Spirit who is in you, whom you have from God, and that you are not your own?

20 For you have been bought with a price: therefore glorify God in your body.

1 JOHN 1:5–9

5 This is the message we have heard from Him and announce to you, that God is Light, and in Him there is no darkness at all.

6 If we say that we have fellowship with Him and yet walk in the darkness, we lie and do not practice the truth;

• Discuss what this and the preceding passage mean in the life of a believer and how the truths revealed here should impact our lifestyles.

OBSERVE

Have you made a mess of your life? Do you feel unworthy of God's love?

Leader: Read 1 John 1:5–9, Psalm 32:5, and Proverbs 28:13 aloud. Have the group do the following:

- *Draw a slash through the words **sin,** **iniquity,** and **transgressions,** like this:*
- *Mark every reference to **God,** including pronouns and synonyms, with a triangle, like this:*
- *Circle the word **fellowship.***

INSIGHT

To *confess our sins* means much more than to simply "admit" them. The word *confess* actually means "to say the same thing about." So to confess your sin means to say the same thing about it that God says about it.

DISCUSS

• What did you learn about fellowship from this passage? How can we enjoy fellowship with God?

• Discuss what you learned from marking the references to sin.

• How should we deal with our sin?

• When we confess our sins, what does God promise and what is the result? Explain your answer.

7 but if we walk in the Light as He Himself is in the Light, we have fellowship with one another, and the blood of Jesus His Son cleanses us from all sin.

8 If we say that we have no sin, we are deceiving ourselves and the truth is not in us.

9 If we confess our sins, He is faithful and righteous to forgive us our sins and to cleanse us from all unrighteousness.

PSALM 32:5

I acknowledged my sin to You, and my iniquity I did not hide; I said, "I will confess my transgressions to the LORD"; and You forgave the guilt of my sin.

PROVERBS 28:13

He who conceals his transgressions will not prosper, but he who confesses and forsakes them will find compassion.

EPHESIANS 5:3–10

3 But immorality or any impurity or greed must not even be named among you, as is proper among saints;

4 and there must be no filthiness and silly talk, or coarse jesting, which are not fitting, but rather giving of thanks.

5 For this you know with certainty, that no immoral or impure person or covetous man, who is an idolater, has an inheritance

• Just so you don't miss it, God not only forgives our sin but what else does He do and what does that mean?

• What happens to the shame and the guilt?

OBSERVE

Once you have confessed your sin and God has forgiven and cleansed you, what are you to do?

Leader: Read Ephesians 5:3–10 aloud. Have the group say aloud and...
   • *mark the word* **immorality** *with a big* **I.**
   • *mark the word* **impurity** *with a big* **X.**
   • *double underline the phrase* **walk as children of light.**

DISCUSS

• Discuss what you learned from marking *immorality* and *impurity*.

• What did you learn about the lifestyle of Christians versus the people of the world in verses 3–7? Compare that with what you have learned in previous lessons.

• How would violating these principles affect your testimony?

• According to verse 8, what were you and what are you now? What command is given here?

• Look closely at verses 9 and 10. What characterizes someone who walks as a child of Light?

in the kingdom of Christ and God.

6 Let no one deceive you with empty words, for because of these things the wrath of God comes upon the sons of disobedience.

7 Therefore do not be partakers with them;

8 for you were formerly darkness, but now you are Light in the Lord; walk as children of Light

9 (for the fruit of the Light consists in all goodness and righteousness and truth),

10 trying to learn what is pleasing to the Lord.

WRAP IT UP

We have seen clearly that sex is God's invention. It is He who created human beings male and female, He who told Adam and Eve to be fruitful and to multiply, and also He who said sex was designed for our pleasure. However, too many have bought into Satan's lies about sex and then discovered to their great regret that God set limits on sex to protect us from the destructive consequences of its misuse.

Have you made a mess of your life because of your sexual choices? Do you feel unworthy of the Father's love? Dirty? Worthless?

Having seen for yourself what God says, do you realize that no matter what you have done, you can be assured of complete and absolute forgiveness? Even if you have been involved in sexually immoral behavior, including sex outside of marriage, oral sex, heavy petting or fondling, incest, adultery, homosexuality, lesbianism, bestiality, or pornography—you *can* be forgiven. "How?" you ask.

1. First, **agree with God that you have sinned—broken His holy Law, rebelled against His holy will.** Name your sins for what they are. The word *confess* in 1 John 1:9 means "to say the same thing." To confess sin, then, is to agree with God that what you have done is wrong.

2. **Take responsibility for your sins.** You can't blame anyone else. Acknowledge your sins and take full responsibility.

3. **Thank God for the blood of Jesus Christ, which cleanses you from all sin, and in faith accept His forgiveness.** Remember, forgiveness is always based on grace, never some-

thing earned. "Where sin abounded, grace did much more abound" (Romans 5:20, KJV).

4. **Take God at His Word.** "Therefore there is now no condemnation for those who are in Christ Jesus" (Romans 8:1). No matter your feelings, cling in faith to what God says. Don't let Satan, the accuser of the brethren, rob you of you of faith's victory.

5. **Thank God for the gift of His Holy Spirit and tell Him that you want to walk by the Spirit so that you will not fulfill the lusts of the flesh** (Galatians 5:16). Prayers like this show genuine repentance.[2]

Scripture challenges us to both believe what God says and to change our behavior accordingly. In reality your belief system always determines your behavior. You have seen what God says about sex; will you now choose to believe it, walk in it, and teach it?

---

[2] If you or someone you know is struggling with this issue, we recommend the 40-Minute study *Forgiveness: Breaking the Power of the Past.*

No-Homework
That Help You

40 MINUTE BIBLE STUDIES

Being a Disciple: Counting the Real Cost
Kay Arthur, Tom & Jane Hart

Building a Marriage That Really Works
Kay Arthur, David & BJ Lawson

How to Make Choices You Won't Regret
Kay Arthur, David & BJ Lawson

A Man's Strategy For Conquering Temptation
Bob Vereen

Living Victoriously in Difficult Times
Kay Arthur, Bob & Diane Vereen

Discovering What the Future Holds
Kay Arthur & Georg Huber

Key Principles of Biblical Fasting
Kay Arthur & Pete De Lacy

Forgiveness: Breaking the Power of the Past
Kay Arthur, David & BJ Lawson

Bible Studies
Discover Truth For Yourself

A 6-WEEK, NO-HOMEWORK BIBLE STUDY
MORE THAN 700,000 SOLD IN THE SERIES

How Do You Know God's Your Father?

Kay Arthur, David & BJ Lawson

PRECEPT MINISTRIES INTERNATIONAL

40minute BIBLE STUDY

A 6-WEEK, NO-HOMEWORK BIBLE STUDY
MORE THAN 700,000 SOLD IN THE SERIES

How Do You Walk the Walk You Talk?

Kay Arthur

PRECEPT MINISTRIES INTERNATIONAL

40minute BIBLE STUDY

A 6-WEEK, NO-HOMEWORK BIBLE STUDY
MORE THAN 700,000 SOLD IN THE SERIES

Money and Possessions: The Quest for Contentment

Kay Arthur & David Arthur

PRECEPT MINISTRIES INTERNATIONAL

40minute BIBLE STUDY

A 6-WEEK, NO-HOMEWORK BIBLE STUDY
MORE THAN 700,000 SOLD IN THE SERIES

The Essentials of Effective Prayer

Kay Arthur, David & BJ Lawson

PRECEPT MINISTRIES INTERNATIONAL

40minute BIBLE STUDY

A 6-WEEK, NO-HOMEWORK BIBLE STUDY
MORE THAN 700,000 SOLD IN THE SERIES

Having a Real Relationship with God

Kay Arthur

PRECEPT MINISTRIES INTERNATIONAL

40minute BIBLE STUDY

A 6-WEEK, NO-HOMEWORK BIBLE STUDY
MORE THAN 700,000 SOLD IN THE SERIES

Rising to the Call of Leadership

Kay Arthur, David & BJ Lawson

PRECEPT MINISTRIES INTERNATIONAL

40minute BIBLE STUDY

A 6-WEEK, NO-HOMEWORK BIBLE STUDY
MORE THAN 700,000 SOLD IN THE SERIES

What Does the Bible Say About Sex?

Kay Arthur, David & BJ Lawson

PRECEPT MINISTRIES INTERNATIONAL

40minute BIBLE STUDY

A 6-WEEK, NO-HOMEWORK BIBLE STUDY
MORE THAN 700,000 SOLD IN THE SERIES

Living a Life of True Worship

Kay Arthur, Bob & Diane Vereen

PRECEPT MINISTRIES INTERNATIONAL

40minute BIBLE STUDY

Another powerful study series
from beloved Bible teacher

LORD, Where Are You When Bad Things Happen?

A Devotional Study on Living by Faith

KAY ARTHUR

LORD, Only You Can Change Me

A Devotional Study on Growing in Character from the Beatitudes

KAY ARTHUR

LORD, Is It Warfare? Teach Me to Stand

A Devotional Study on Spiritual Victory

KAY ARTHUR

LORD, I Want to Know You

A Devotional Study on the Names of God

KAY ARTHUR

LORD, I Need Grace to Make It Today

A Devotional Study on God's Power for Daily Living

KAY ARTHUR

KAY ARTHUR

The Lord series provides insightful, warm-hearted Bible studies designed to meet you where you are —and help you discover God's answers to your deepest needs.

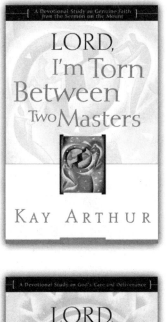

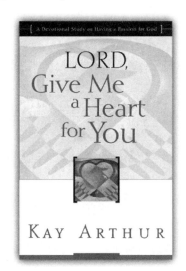

ALSO AVAILABLE:
One-year devotionals to draw you closer to the heart of God.

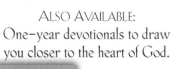

ABOUT KAY ARTHUR AND PRECEPT MINISTRIES INTERNATIONAL

KAY ARTHUR is known around the world as an international Bible teacher, author, conference speaker, and host of the national radio and television programs *Precepts for Life,* which reaches a worldwide viewing audience of over 94 million. A four-time Gold Medallion Award–winning author, Kay has authored more than 100 books and Bible studies.

Kay and her husband, Jack, founded Precept Ministries International in 1970 in Chattanooga, Tennessee, with a vision to establish people in God's Word. Today, the ministry has a worldwide outreach. In addition to inductive study training workshops and thousands of small-group studies across America, PMI reaches nearly 150 countries with inductive Bible studies translated into nearly 70 languages, teaching people to discover Truth for themselves.

Contact Precept Ministries International for more information about inductive Bible studies in your area.

Precept Ministries International
P.O. Box 182218
Chattanooga, TN 37422-7218
800-763-8280
www.precept.org

ABOUT DAVID AND BJ LAWSON

DAVID AND BJ LAWSON have been involved with Precept Ministries International since 1980. After nine years in the pastorate, they joined PMI full-time as directors of the student ministries and staff teachers and trainers. A featured speaker at PMI conferences and in Precept Upon Precept videos, David writes for the Precept Upon Precept series, the New Inductive Study Series, and the 40-Minute Bible Studies series. BJ has written numerous 40-Minute Bible Studies and serves as the chief editor and developer of the series. In addition she is a featured speaker at PMI women's conferences.